THE ES

Guidebook

DEEANNA MERZ NAGEL
MADISON LEIGH AKRIDGE

ILLUSTRATED BY
LIA LITTLEWOOD

FLOWER of LIFE PRESS

The Essential Soul Care™ Oracle Guidebook

The content of this book is for general instruction only. Each person's physical, emotional, and spiritual condition is unique. The instruction in this book is not intended to replace or interrupt the reader's relationship with a physician or other mental health professional. Please consult your doctor for matters pertaining to your specific health.

Published by Flower of Life Press, Old Saybrook, CT
To contact the publisher, visit floweroflifepress.com

Guidebook design by Kirsten Livingston
Artwork by Lia Littlewood

Library of Congress Control Number: Available Upon Request

ISBN-13: 978-1-7371839-4-5

Printed in the United States of America

Contents

The Essential Soul Care Oracle

Guidebook

~

To our teachers, mentors, clients,
students, family and Soul Tribe
who have acted as Muses along
our path, we honor you.

~

What is Essential Soul Care?

Essential Soul Care is simply that... Essential Care for the Soul.

Each card is an extension of the 7 elements of soul expansion and the corresponding 7 primary chakras.

7 Elements	7 Chakras
Transcendence	Crown
Intuition	Third Eye
Mindset	Throat
Community	Heart
Nourishment	Solar Plexus
Creativity	Sacral
Sanctuary	Root

The Essential Soul Care™ Guidebook

~

Why we created the Essential Soul Care™ Oracle Guidebook

This guidebook offers essential information about soul care. The guidebook was created to stand alone or as a companion to the Essential Soul Care Oracle deck.

~

How to Use This Guidebook

If you wish to use the guidebook as a sole point of reference, we recommend utilizing the guidebook as a grounding and centering tool. The journal prompts can be used to engage in contemplative writing as described further along in the introduction pages. We encourage you to read the full introduction even if you do not intend to use the deck. This additional pertinent information will be beneficial as you traverse onto this spiritual journey.

~

49-day Essential Soul Care™ Cleanse

Take this guidebook in sequence, referencing a card each day. Make use of crystals and essential oils as you desire. Repeat the mantra sounds and affirmation. Engage in contemplative writing for both the Soul Play prompts and the Soul Work prompts. Begin the next day's writing with reflection on any synchronicities from the day before.

~

Essential Soul Care™ Page Flip

Ask for Divine guidance and open the guidebook to any random page. You can follow the 1-3-4-5 or 7 card spread instructions and flip the pages just once or several times depending on the spread you choose. The difference between using the guidebook without the deck is that you would engage in both the soul play and soul work prompts.

♥

Color charts and additional resources are available at the **essentialsoul.care** website

Why We Created the Essential Soul Care™ Oracle

The deck was created to act as the Oracle. Oracle decks are a form of divination and the messages herein have been illuminated through the authors directly from Source. Regardless of your faith expression, the messages can stand alone as a singular process or complement your own spiritual path. You will discover beliefs and artifacts from other spiritual cultures throughout the guidebook and deck. These discoveries are touchpoints for you to further explore if you so desire.

The authors have a combined 40 years of experience in the field of psychotherapy, coaching, energy healing, aromatherapy and other various areas of the healing arts. We blended our knowledge and intuitive gifts to channel a deck that embodies the many elements of well-being. This deck serves as a guide when you are seeking discernment from your inner voice, your Higher Self or from Spirit.

♥

How to Use the Deck

Preparing the Deck

Please know that you can prepare your deck in whatever way speaks to you. The authors use the following methods to prepare and anoint a deck for use:

- Hold the deck in one hand and tap the full deck with the other hand to clear the energy from packaging and shipping.
- Place a drop of your favorite essential oil in the palms of your hands and rub together then open the deck and shuffle.
- Touch each card. Get to know the deck. Become familiar with the artistry, the words, the vibration of the deck.
- Make the deck YOUR Oracle. This does not mean others can't touch your deck. That is a personal choice.
- After you receive the deck, you can prepare the deck immediately by placing the cards in a bowl or large plate and sprinkling Himalyan salt over the cards to clear any residual energy.
- During a Full Moon cycle, you may also place the deck outside for a moon bath.

Card Layout

The *front-facing* card shows a mandala with 7 elements of soul expansion. Each element harmonizes with a specific chakra.

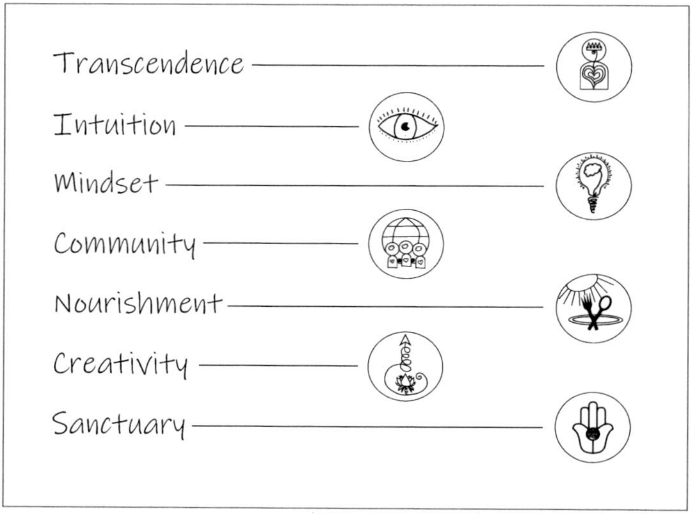

The mandala represents the Essential Soul Care Wellness Wheel and is a reminder of the Circle of Life.

The ***back-facing*** cards offer the Oracle's theme, keywords and an illustration. Once you are accustomed to the deck, just seeing the image and a few keywords may trigger a message the Oracle has for you. And of course, this booklet also contains further exploration for each card.

The cards are also color-coded according to the chakras:

Violet – Crown

Indigo – Third Eye

Blue – Throat

Green – Heart

Yellow – Solar Plexus

Orange – Sacral

Red – Root

~

Card Descriptions

The card descriptions contained within this booklet repeat the Oracle's theme and keywords as well as the corresponding element and chakra, followed by the Oracle Message.

Once you have read the Oracle Message, your Soul Play begins.

~ Anoint the chakra with the suggested ***Essential Oil*** while setting your intention with the *Affirmation*. If you do not have the essential oil recommended, use whatever essential oil you have on hand or what your intuition leads you to use. Good quality essential oils carry a positive vibration. For essential oil safety guidelines, see essentialsoul.care.

Soul Play includes the following components:

Essential Oil

Crystal

Chakra Mantra

Affirmation

Journal Prompt

~

- ~ Bring your ***Crystal*** to your reading. Use your intuition when deciding how you prefer to connect with the crystal. Here are some suggestions: hold it, set it next to you, set it next to the cards. Gaze at or hold the crystal for a moment and invite the vibration of the crystal to add depth and value to your reading.
- ~ Activate the targeted chakra by vocalizing the *Chakra Mantra*. As your voice emits the Chakra Mantra, the vibration that occurs will resonate throughout your mind/body/spirit and will set the intention for the targeted chakra to receive input.

The *Journal Prompt* is your path toward expansion. Write whatever comes to mind using *Contemplative Writing*. Contemplative writing is a highly effective tool that opens communication between your conscious, cognitive mind (left-brain) and the unconscious, intuitive mind (right-brain), or, said differently, between your ego and your soul.

Set a specific period of time aside for your journal experience. This might be 2 mins, 5 mins or 10 mins, depending on how comfortable you are with the idea of writing, or how much you think you have to say. Once you have developed or enhanced this skill, you can increase the time that you choose to allocate to contemplative writing.

Settle into a comfortable environment, one that is well-lit, warm or cool (depending on what your body needs) and preferably one where you will not be interrupted mid-contemplation!

~

Reversed Card Reading

When a card shows up in reverse, you are asked to go deeper. Following the *Soul Play*, you will then engage in *Soul Study*.

Soul Study represents the shadow side; the shadow shows up as a challenge that may be playing out with a negative impact in your life. The Soul Study journal prompt is the shadow spin of the Soul Play journal prompt.

Use the same contemplative writing technique with the Soul Study journal prompt as you did with the Soul Play journal prompt.

Following the Soul Study journal prompt you will see a couple of words or phrases representing ***Defining Moments***. These are topics or items to dive deeper for an expanded awareness of the card. You are encouraged to study these terms and learn more about the Oracle's message. As with the card messages, the Defining Moments represent inclusivity from an interfaith and multifaith perspective and are included to expand your understanding and knowledge base. That we have not included all faith perspective is only because of the limits of the 49 cards. Expect more in our future works.

~

Card Spreads

When asking a question of the Oracle, try to keep a short timeline. For a one-card or 3-card spread, ask in terms of the day at hand or, "for the next 24-hour period." When asking for broader information in a larger spread, you may consider a longer period of time but know that free will can come into play at any point. Keeping the questions to a shorter timeline also avoids "future-casting." The Oracle does not act as a predictor but rather, serves as your spiritual guide.

While most oracle and tarot decks give a demonstration as to how to lay out the cards when pulled, Essential Soul Care spreads are meant to tap into your intuition. Play with the spreads and feel free to use your own unique placement (such as in a row, bridge, cross, or in a random manner).

Jumper Cards

If a card jumps from the deck, intuitively decide whether this card is directly reflective of the question at hand or is offered as a clarification card for the overall reading.

1-CARD DRAW

Pull one card for a general reading, to set an intention for your day, or wrap up your day. You can also pull one card to determine which Essential Soul Care element and corresponding chakra requires special attention at the moment.

3-CARD ESC SPREAD

1. **E**nlightenment: What message does Spirit have for me regarding the question at hand?
2. **S**teps: What action(s) do I need to take now?
3. **C**onclusion: What is my outcome if I consider the enlightenment given and follow the advised steps?

~

4-CARD A&E SPREAD

Abode, **A**bundance, **E**nergy, **E**xpansion: This spread can be used to set intention for your day, week, month, or phase of life. The spread is broken down into 4 areas of your life:

1. **A**bode: Home and Family
2. **A**bundance: Wealth and Finances
3. **E**nergy: Health and Wellness
4. **E**xpansion: Love and Spiritual Connection

Pull one card for each area. Pull all 4 cards in sequence. Lay the cards out in a row or in a square (your choice). If you need clarification, pull an extra card after the first 4 are drawn.

~

5-CARD RELATIONSHIP SPREAD

You, Person of Interest, Enlightenment, Steps, Conclusion: This spread can be used for guidance with any relationship, whether friends, family, co-workers or any other person you are engaged with on any level, whether energetically, physically or otherwise.

1. You: Where am I energetically at the present time?
2. Person of Interest: Where is my POI energetically at the present time?
3. **E**nlightenment: What do I need to know about this connection?
4. **S**teps: What action(s) do I need to take now?
5. **C**onclusion: What is my outcome if I consider the enlightenment given and follow the advised steps?

Pull one card for each area. Pull all 5 cards in sequence. Lay the cards out in order or in a pattern, choosing the first card you pulled as the first area and so forth.

~

7-CARD ESC (ELEMENTAL SYMBOLS/CHAKRAS) SPREAD

This spread is focused on Essential Soul Care's 7 elements of soul expansion. Each element has a corresponding chakra.

1. Transcendence/Crown: Purpose and Spirituality
2. Intuition/Third Eye: Vision, Strategy and Clair Senses
3. Mindset/Throat: Communication and Guidance
4. Community/Heart: Relationships and Healing, Giving and Receiving Love
5. Nourishment/Solar Plexus: Mentality, Self-worth and Structure
6. Creativity/Sacral: Passion and Creativity
7. Sanctuary/Root: Security and Survival

Chakras, Essential Oils, Crystals and Chakra Mantras

CROWN

Body Systems:
Endocrine, Nervous, Immune

Emotional Process:
Purpose and Spirituality

Essential Oil

Frankincense:
Improves communication with source

Crystal

Clear Quartz:
Clarity, Release, Expansion

Chakra Mantra

AH (A-A-A-H-H-H)

THIRD EYE

Body Systems:
Endocrine, Nervous, Visual, Olfactory

Emotional Process:
Vision, Strategy and Clair Senses

Essential Oil

Basil:
Creates an open mind and clarity of thought

Crystal

Amethyst:
Transformation, Intuition, Relaxation

Chakra Mantra

OM (A-A-A-U-U-M)

~

THROAT

Body Systems:
Endocrine, Musculoskeletal, Lymphatic, Throat & Mouth, Auditory

Emotional Process:
Communication and Guidance

Essential Oil

Cistus:
Simulates the senses of touch, sight and sound

Crystal

Lapis Lazuli:
Truth, Wisdom, Self-Expression

Chakra Mantra

HAM (H-A-A-A-M)

HEART

Body Systems:
Cardiovascular, Respiratory,
Breasts, Musculoskeletal

Emotional Process:
Relationships and Healing, Giving
and Receiving Love

Essential Oil

Geranium:
Brings a sense of joy, well-being,
emotional balance and hope

Crystal

Aventurine:
Compassion, Empathy, Prosperity

Chakra Mantra

YAM (Y-A-A-A-M):

~

SOLAR PLEXUS

Body Systems:
Digestive, Renal, Musculoskeletal

Emotional Process:
Mentality, Self-Worth and Structure

Essential Oil

Juniper:
Evokes feelings of health, love and peace

Crystal

Tiger Eye:
Courage, Personal Power, Confidence

Chakra Mantra

RAM (R-A-A-A-M)

SACRAL

Body Systems:
Reproductive, Renal, Adrenal (endocrine)

Emotional Process:
Passion and Creativity

Essential Oil

Vetiver:
Sexual energies become more peaceful and grounded

Crystal

Carnelian:
Motivation, Vitality, Fertility

Chakra Mantra

VAM (V-A-A-A-M)

ROOT

Body Systems:
Skin, Coccyx (Musculoskeletal), Reproductive

Emotional Process:
Security and Survival

Essential Oil

Cypress:
Strengthens, centers and heals emotions

Crystal

Red Jasper:
Stability, Security, Grounding

Chakra Mantra

LAM (L-A-A-A-M)

Color charts and additional resources are available at the **essentialsoul.care** website

The Essential Soul Care Oracle

Guidebook

1

Circle of Life

Birth ~ Being ~ Death

~

Transcendence
Crown Chakra

~

The Oracle Message
The Circle of Life card appears to remind you that life is precious. Every life has a beginning and an end and ultimately comes full-circle. How you choose to spend your time and energy while in this space determines the quality of your life now. Connect to your Higher Self as you navigate the world in the most optimal way.

SOUL PLAY

Essential Oil

Frankincense

Crystal

Clear Quartz

Repeat this **Chakra Mantra** for 30 seconds:

AH (A-A-A-H-H-H)

Repeat this **Affirmation** three times:

I trust the process of life.

Journal Prompt

How can you honor and embrace life in new ways?

~

SOUL STUDY

Journal Prompt

How does your fear of the unknown keep you from living your best life now?

Defining Moments

Mandala ~ Enso

2

Contemplation

Divination ~ Conversation ~ Prayer

~

Transcendence
Crown Chakra

~

The Oracle Message

God is calling. Are you dialed in? Contemplation, divination, meditation and prayer are but some of the ways in which you can converse with the One. You can answer the call and listen or begin the conversation and be heard. It is a two way street.

SOUL PLAY

Essential Oil

Frankincense

Crystal

Clear Quartz

Repeat this **Chakra Mantra**
for 30 seconds:

AH (A-A-A-H-H-H)

Repeat this **Affirmation**
three times:

Information from Source comes to me readily.

Journal Prompt

In what ways do you communicate with the Divine?

~

SOUL STUDY

Journal Prompt

What keeps you from having rich and meaningful dialogue with the One?

Defining Moments

Divination ~ Contemplative Prayer

3

Peaceful Council

Ask ~ Reveal ~ Allow

~

Transcendence

Crown Chakra

~

The Oracle Message

The dove is a spirit messenger. You are being reminded to rely on your guides. Ancestors, ascended masters, totems, ethereal and celestial beings are available to you. Ask Source to reveal your spiritual mentors and allow. Remember too, your Higher Self is also part of your council.

SOUL PLAY

Essential Oil

Frankincense

Crystal

Clear Quartz

Repeat this **Chakra Mantra** for 30 seconds:

AH (A-A-A-H-H-H)

Repeat this **Affirmation** three times:

I am Divinely guided.

Journal Prompt

Who is part of your peaceful council?

~

SOUL STUDY

Journal Prompt

Describe a circumstance that might have been experienced differently had you trusted your Higher Self.

Defining Moments

Ascended Masters ~ Totem Animal

4

Fields of Gold

Aura ~ Illumination ~ Radiance

~

Transcendence

Crown Chakra

~

The Oracle Message

You have a luminous energy field, or aura, that radiates from your inner being. Just as illuminating as a lustrous field of golden wheat on a sunny day, your chi, or life force energy is brilliant and far-reaching. This glowing essence comes from Divine Source and emanates from your higher self. Bask in the warmth of this life-giving energy.

SOUL PLAY

Essential Oil

Frankincense

Crystal

Clear Quartz

Repeat this **Chakra Mantra** for 30 seconds:

AH (A-A-A-H-H-H)

Repeat this **Affirmation** three times:

My energy field is luminous.

Journal Prompt

Describe your own radiant aura.

~

SOUL STUDY

Journal Prompt

Describe a time when you would have benefited from allowing the light to come in.

Defining Moments

Prana ~ Shakti

5

This Is the Dawning

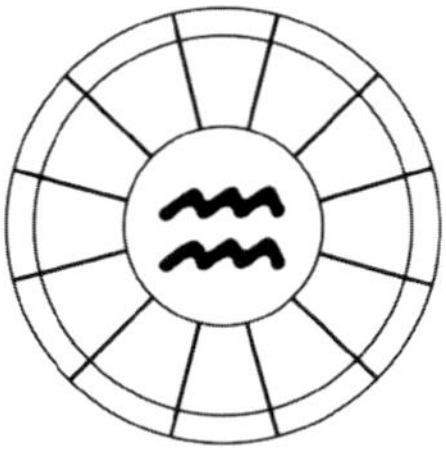

Harmony ~ Benevolence ~ Empathy

Transcendence
Crown Chakra

The Oracle Message

The Age of Aquarius is upon us. You are living in a time when the Divine Feminine and Divine Masculine are finding harmony. This means the Divine You. Your yin and yang are calling for balance. Empathy and benevolence exist between the anima and animus.

SOUL PLAY

Essential Oil

Frankincense

Crystal

Clear Quartz

Repeat this **Chakra Mantra** for 30 seconds:

AH (A-A-A-H-H-H)

Repeat this **Affirmation** three times:

I am a Divine being.

Journal Prompt

How do you experience the yin and yang balance within?

~

SOUL STUDY

Journal Prompt

When do you feel the tug between the Divine Feminine and the Divine Masculine both within and around you?

Defining Moments

Yin/Yang ~ Anima/Animus

6

Let It Shine

Source ~ Guidance ~ Light

~

Transcendence
Crown Chakra

~

The Oracle Message
You are filled with light from Source. This light ignites each of your chakras, going up from your crown chakra into the ethers, down from your root chakra to the earth's core, and out from your heart chakra into the vast space before you. Peaceful guidance unfolds in this light. Be a beacon so others can find their way.

SOUL PLAY

Essential Oil

Frankincense

Crystal

Clear Quartz

Repeat this **Chakra Mantra** for 30 seconds:

AH (A-A-A-H-H-H)

Repeat this **Affirmation** three times:

I am a source of love and light.

Journal Prompt

How do you best shine your light?

~

SOUL STUDY

Journal Prompt

What experiences in the past have caused your light to go dim?

Defining Moments

Christ Consciousness ~ Violet Flame

7

The Great Beyond

Afterlife ~ Heaven ~ Rebirth

~

Transcendence

Crown Chakra

~

The Oracle Message

Death is a part of living yet many of us fear it so—for ourselves and for others. This card is showing up to remind you of the great beyond. Once you pass over, you celebrate a new beginning and those left behind become Earth angels who celebrate your new celestial birth. Isn't that lovely?

SOUL PLAY

Essential Oil

Frankincense

Crystal

Clear Quartz

Repeat this **Chakra Mantra** for 30 seconds:

AH (A-A-A-H-H-H)

Repeat this **Affirmation** three times:

I am stardust.

Journal Prompt

How do thoughts of an afterlife soothe you?

~

SOUL STUDY

Journal Prompt

Dust to dust. What about death do you fear?

Defining Moments

Thanatology ~ Near-death Experience (NDE)

8

Sacred Evolution

Unfolding ~ Remembering ~ Rejoining

~

Intuition

Third Eye Chakra

~

The Oracle Message

The Unalome shows that your path is unfolding before you. You came into this world to discover your innate talents and gifts. This involves navigating twists and turns, ultimately remembering and rejoining your highest and truest self. The journey is one of continuous movement toward enlightenment.

SOUL PLAY

Essential Oil

Basil

Crystal

Amethyst

Repeat this **Chakra Mantra**
for 30 seconds:

OM (A-A-A-U-U-M)

Repeat this **Affirmation**
three times:

I am on the path of self-discovery.

Journal Prompt

What next steps would you like to take?

~

SOUL STUDY

Journal Prompt

What obstacles need removing
from your path?

Defining Moments

Unalome ~ Dharma

9

Take It In

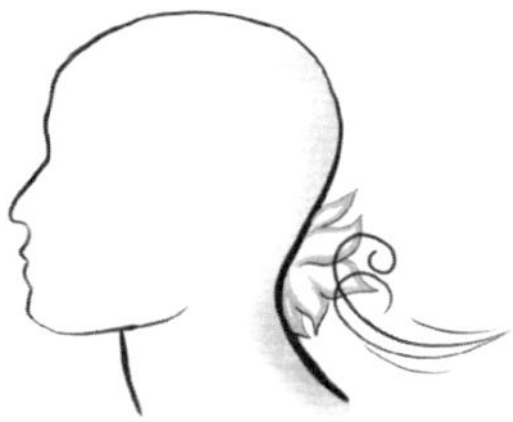

Intuition ~ Clairvoyance ~ Clearing

~

Intuition
Third Eye Chakra

~

The Oracle Message

When we draw in source energy, filling our being with white light, we can choose to bring the light in from the crown or from the Mouth of God. From the medulla, the light reaches our third eye. See what is before you. Your intuition is speaking.

SOUL PLAY

Essential Oil

Basil

Crystal

Amethyst

Repeat this **Chakra Mantra** for 30 seconds:

OM (A-A-A-U-U-M)

Repeat this **Affirmation** three times:

My third eye sees all.

Journal Prompt

When you bring Source energy directly to your third eye, what is your full view?

~

SOUL STUDY

Journal Prompt

Your view is distorted.
What can you do to lift the fog?

Defining Moments

Mouth of God ~ Ananda

10

Across Space and Time

Healing ~ Lightwork ~ Vibration

~

Intuition

Third Eye Chakra

~

The Oracle Message

Use energetic intention with others. Trust that your good vibes travel across space and time, through the interwebs and across continents. Whether we are physical or non-local, in the same room or across the globe, prayer and exchange of healing energies work. Activate the healer within.

SOUL PLAY

Essential Oil

Basil

Crystal

Amethyst

Repeat this **Chakra Mantra** for 30 seconds:

OM (A-A-A-U-U-M)

Repeat this **Affirmation** three times:

I am open to my intuitive and healing abilities.

Journal Prompt

When you pray or send light to others, how are you nurtured in the process?

~

SOUL STUDY

Journal Prompt

Pay attention to your intuition. Are you being a clear channel or is ego/agenda getting in the way?

Defining Moments

Energy Medicine ~ Kybernetes Reiki

11

Curtain Call

Clairaudience ~ Mediumship ~ Extrasensory

Intuition

Third Eye Chakra

The Oracle Message

Spirit exists in the in-between. This is where the veil is thin. Spirits are among us. Death is not the final curtain call. Loved ones reach across the cosmic divide to give us messages of love and light. Others may show up for assistance with passing over. Listen with your third ear.

SOUL PLAY

Essential Oil

Basil

Crystal

Amethyst

Repeat this **Chakra Mantra**
for 30 seconds:

OM (A-A-A-U-U-M)

Repeat this **Affirmation**
three times:

I hear with my third eye.

Journal Prompt

What message(s) have you heard from the other side?

~

SOUL STUDY

Journal Prompt

How does fear and logic keep you from communicating with those who have already passed over?

Defining Moments

Thin Veil ~ Psychopomp

12

Timing Is Everything

Decisions ~ Choices ~ Outcomes

~

Intuition

Third Eye Chakra

~

The Oracle Message

The time is now. That is all we have—NOW. How we choose to respond to offers, opportunities or circumstances from moment to moment directly correlates to the outcome we experience. Choosing not to respond is also a decision. Trusting Divine Timing will lead to a desirable outcome, regardless.

SOUL PLAY

Essential Oil

Basil

Crystal

Amethyst

Repeat this **Chakra Mantra** for 30 seconds:

OM (A-A-A-U-U-M)

Repeat this **Affirmation** three times:

I use my intuition to choose if and when to respond.

Journal Prompt

Recall a time you felt Divine Timing was at play.

~

SOUL STUDY

Journal Prompt

When do you feel the most pressure to make hasty decisions?

Defining Moments

Divine Timing ~ Free Will

13

Overshadowed

Eclipse ~ Lessons ~ Resilience

~

Intuition

Third Eye Chakra

~

The Oracle Message

This too shall pass. When your light goes dim, there is shadow work to do. There are times when even the sun appears to be muted and snuffed out during a cloudy day or eclipse cycle, yet the sun continues to shine underneath it all. Trust that once the lesson is learned, your light will shine on and you can bask in the glow of your resilience.

SOUL PLAY

Essential Oil

Basil

Crystal

Amethyst

Repeat this **Chakra Mantra** for 30 seconds:

OM (A-A-A-U-U-M)

Repeat this **Affirmation** three times:

My soul's light is ever-glowing.

Journal Prompt

Reflect on a time when you allowed the dark clouds to pass.

~

SOUL STUDY

Journal Prompt

What lies in the shadows for you now?

Defining Moments

Eclipse Season ~ Cloud Meditation

14

In Safe Keeping

Protection ~ Restoration ~ Vitality

~

Intuition
Third Eye Chakra

~

The Oracle Message

The Universe has your back. The Eye of Horus has emerged to provide protection, restorative healing and renewed vitality. This "all seeing eye" keeps you in its scope as you move about your days freely without fear.

SOUL PLAY

Essential Oil

Basil

Crystal

Amethyst

Repeat this **Chakra Mantra** for 30 seconds:

OM (A-A-A-U-U-M)

Repeat this **Affirmation** three times:

I welcome protection, vitality and healing for my highest and best good.

Journal Prompt

How do you know when you're thriving?

~

SOUL STUDY

Journal Prompt

What would you do if you weren't afraid?

Defining Moments

Eye of Horus ~ Eye of Ra

15

True Blue

Truth ~ Freedom ~ Authenticity

Mindset

Throat Chakra

The Oracle Message

When Whale energy appears, you are being called to free your mind and speak your truth. Being authentic and transparent in how you feel and what you say creates a calmness, yet empowered sense of being. Yes means Yes. No means No. No apologies needed. The truth shall set you free.

SOUL PLAY

Essential Oil

Cistus

Crystal

Lapis Lazuli

Repeat this **Chakra Mantra** for 30 seconds:

HAM (H-A-A-A-M)

Repeat this **Affirmation** three times:

I express my truth with ease.

Journal Prompt

What 3 truths do you need or want to express?

~

SOUL STUDY

Journal Prompt

When do you tend to say YES when you really want to say NO?

Defining Moments

Whale Symbolism ~ Spirit Animal

16

Everyone Has a Story

Edit ~ Turnabout ~ Rescript

Mindset

Throat Chakra

The Oracle Message

When Rabbit appears, he's there to help you pivot and change course, as White Rabbit did with Alice during her spiritual awakening. The stories we are told growing up weave into the fabric of our current reality. Were all the stories true? If not, it's never too late to edit them and write your current stories with a renewed understanding of how you want your life to now unfold.

SOUL PLAY

Essential Oil

Cistus

Crystal

Lapis Lazuli

Repeat this **Chakra Mantra** for 30 seconds:

HAM (H-A-A-A-M)

Repeat this **Affirmation** three times:

I am writing this chapter of my life on my terms.

Journal Prompt

What is the thread of truth that you want to keep as part of your life story?

~

SOUL STUDY

Journal Prompt

What story in your book of life needs fact-checking?

Defining Moments

White Rabbit ~ Life Script

17

Sands of Time

Akasha ~ Reincarnation ~ Karma

~

Mindset

Throat Chakra

~

The Oracle Message

The hourglass is always full of sifting sand. Our souls span many lifetimes and we bring forth accumulated lessons learned in each new incarnation. Akashic records represent your book of life held in the universal etheric field. Understanding the history and provenance of your stories is a courageous act that leads to your personal truth.

SOUL PLAY

Essential Oil

Cistus

Crystal

Lapis Lazuli

Repeat this **Chakra Mantra** for 30 seconds:

HAM (H-A-A-A-M)

Repeat this **Affirmation** three times:

I speak with clarity, compassion, and courage.

Journal Prompt

What courageous life lessons have you learned that influence your personal truth?

~

SOUL STUDY

Journal Prompt

Fear of discovering your past is keeping you from right now. What can you do to release the fear and be open to the lessons?

Defining Moments

Akashic Record ~ Samsāra

18

Express Yourself

Harmony ~ Congruence ~ Coherence

~

Mindset

Throat Chakra

~

The Oracle Message

Congruence = Harmony. When our hearts and brains are in conflict, we experience a discord that shuts down our ability to speak our truth. Place your Left hand on your head and your Right hand on your heart to create a circuit of energy flow. This movement will help activate your throat chakra so you may find your harmonious voice again.

SOUL PLAY

Essential Oil

Cistus

Crystal

Lapis Lazuli

Repeat this **Chakra Mantra**
for 30 seconds:

HAM (H-A-A-A-M)

Repeat this **Affirmation**
three times:

*My heart and brain work together
so I may speak my ultimate truth.*

Journal Prompt

Do the heart/brain exercise described in the Oracle's message and write about your experience.

~

SOUL STUDY

Journal Prompt

What happens to your ultimate truth when you are only "following your heart" or "in your head?"

Defining Moments

Cognitive Dissonance ~ Congruence

19

Dark Horse

Shadow ~ Light ~ Emergence

~

Mindset

Throat Chakra

~

The Oracle Message

The Dark Horse is a noble and courageous animal that emerges out of the shadows and reigns victorious. A powerful contender, the dark horse faces fears, steps into the light and perseveres throughout its journey. Now is the time to acknowledge your shadow self, be open to the message Spirit is bringing you and use your inner voice to follow your integrity as you travel into the light.

SOUL PLAY

Essential Oil

Cistus

Crystal

Lapis Lazuli

Repeat this **Chakra Mantra**
for 30 seconds:

HAM (H-A-A-A-M)

Repeat this **Affirmation**
three times:

Where there is darkness, there is also light.

Journal Prompt

*Describe what brought you light
after you experienced darkness.*

~

SOUL STUDY

Journal Prompt

*How does your Shadow-Side
keep you from seeing the light?*

Defining Moments

Dark Night of the Soul ~ Shadow Work

20

Read Between the Lines

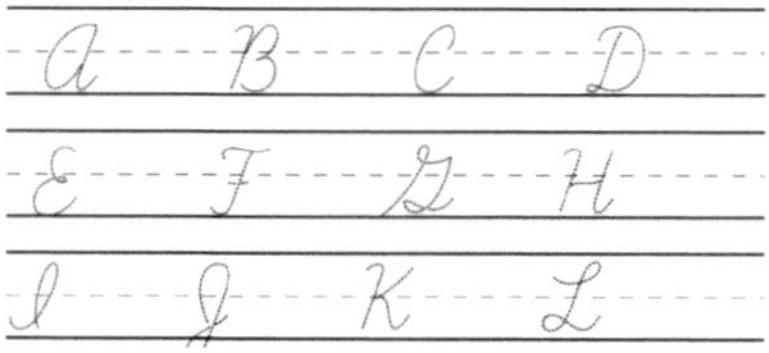

Reception ~ Compassion ~ Wisdom

Mindset

Throat Chakra

The Oracle Message

Hear the full story. Give attention to all of your Clairs before you speak so that your words are a gift. When you lean in to another with deep, sacred listening first, you will respond with a clear message that can be received as sage enlightenment.

SOUL PLAY

Essential Oil

Cistus

Crystal

Lapis Lazuli

Repeat this **Chakra Mantra**
for 30 seconds:

HAM (H-A-A-A-M)

Repeat this **Affirmation**
three times:

*I listen with sacred attention
before I speak.*

Journal Prompt

*When you deeply listen to another, what
is the gift you receive in return?*

~

SOUL STUDY

Journal Prompt

*Describe a situation when you did
not listen for the full story and you were too
quick to give advice.*

Defining Moments

Clair Senses ~ Sacred Listening

21

I'll Fly Away

Accountability ~ Freedom ~ Responsibility

~

Mindset

Throat Chakra

~

The Oracle Message

Taking responsibility let's the caged bird free. Sometimes it feels that you just want to fly away from everything and dodge duty. In actuality, when we accept what we are responsible for, we experience personal freedom that causes us to sing in celebration.

SOUL PLAY

Essential Oil

Cistus

Crystal

Lapis Lazuli

Repeat this **Chakra Mantra**
for 30 seconds:

HAM (H-A-A-A-M)

Repeat this **Affirmation**
three times:

*Being accountable is freeing
and courageous.*

Journal Prompt

*When has taking responsibility
complimented your authentic voice?*

~

SOUL STUDY

Journal Prompt

*Describe a time when dodging
responsibility made you feel like
a caged bird.*

Defining Moments

Existentialism ~ Stoicism

22

Sweet Surrender

Altruism ~ Service ~ Peace

~

Community
Heart Chakra

~

The Oracle Message
Becoming an instrument of peace for the greater good is such sweet surrender. In doing so, we are able to be of service to others with heart-centered compassion. An altruistic approach embodies unconditional love without expectation.

SOUL PLAY

Essential Oil

Geranium

Crystal

Aventurine

Repeat this **Chakra Mantra**
for 30 seconds:

YAM (Y-A-A-A-M)

Repeat this **Affirmation**
three times:

I am fully open to being of service to others.

Journal Prompt

How do you expand when you are of service to others?

~

SOUL STUDY

Journal Prompt

What keeps you from giving whole-heartedly to others?

Defining Moments

Detachment ~ Unconditional Positive Regard

23

Compassionate Prosperity

Generosity ~ Bounty ~ Humanity

~

Community

Heart Chakra

~

The Oracle Message

Lakshmi is the Hindu Goddess of purity, love and wealth. She comes to you today to bring a message of compassionate prosperity as a good samaritan. Having abundance is only the first step to prosperity. Being able to freely and generously give to others in a spirit of compassion and non-attachment is the key to being truly "rich."

SOUL PLAY

Essential Oil

Geranium

Crystal

Aventurine

Repeat this **Chakra Mantra** for 30 seconds:

YAM (Y-A-A-A-M)

Repeat this **Affirmation** three times:

I give of my time and resources to those in need with no strings attached.

Journal Prompt

When you practice compassionate prosperity how do you feel?

~

SOUL STUDY

Journal Prompt

Lack mentality can keep us from prospering and giving back. How has lack mentality shown up in your life?

Defining Moments

Sacred Economics ~ Pay it Forward

24

Born With It

Family ~ Boundaries ~ Acceptance

~

Community

Heart Chakra

~

The Oracle Message

Your family of origin was assigned to you when you arrived here. Family time can be both rewarding and challenging. Establishing healthy boundaries allows for freedom and autonomy while being a part of the whole. It is possible to have firm boundaries and unconditional love simultaneously.

SOUL PLAY

Essential Oil

Geranium

Crystal

Aventurine

Repeat this **Chakra Mantra** for 30 seconds:

YAM (Y-A-A-A-M)

Repeat this **Affirmation** three times:

I am a source of joy and inspiration to my family.

Journal Prompt

In what ways does your family of origin show you unconditional love and acceptance?

~

SOUL STUDY

Journal Prompt

How can you keep your boundaries with your family and give of yourself at the same time?

Defining Moments

Enmeshment ~ Interconnectedness

25

A Grieving Heart

Release ~ Cleanse ~ Breathe

~

Community

Heart Chakra

~

The Oracle Message

Grief is a part of life. Grief is the normal response to loss of any kind. Whether you have lost a loved one, a fur baby, a relationship or a job, the feelings you are having are valid and real. Everyone grieves differently so be gentle with yourself. Your tears are cleansing. Remember to breathe. Place your hand over your heart and just breathe.

SOUL PLAY

Essential Oil

Geranium

Crystal

Aventurine

Repeat this **Chakra Mantra**
for 30 seconds:

YAM (Y-A-A-A-M)

Repeat this **Affirmation**
three times:

My heart feels light today.

Journal Prompt

When have you experienced loving memories that have warmed your heart?

SOUL STUDY

Journal Prompt

Your heavy heart wants to release the grief.
If grief could speak,
what would grief say to you?

Defining Moments

Stages of Grief ~ Rainbow Bridge

26

Birds of a Feather

Kindred ~ Network ~ Collective

~

Community

Heart Chakra

~

The Oracle Message

"Birds of a Feather Flock Together"—an old adage with a timeless message. Like attracts Like. As human beings, we tend to be drawn to people with similar tastes, interests, and values. Finding your Soul Tribe or group of Kindred Spirits can bring great fulfillment and joy to your life. It's time to expand and strengthen your Inner Circle. Seek quality, not quantity when you are building your network.

SOUL PLAY

Essential Oil

Geranium

Crystal

Aventurine

Repeat this **Chakra Mantra**
for 30 seconds:

YAM (Y-A-A-A-M)

Repeat this **Affirmation**
three times:

*My authenticity attracts
authentic people.*

Journal Prompt

What benefits do you receive from being connected to your soul family?

~

SOUL STUDY

Journal Prompt

You are challenged to be inclusive of others. When have you overlooked a connection because the differences were more obvious than the similarities?

Defining Moments

Soul Tribe ~ Inner Circle

27
Dog Days

Loyalty ~ Companionship ~ Presence

~

Community
Heart Chakra

~

The Oracle Message
Dogs are by nature loyal companions. When Dog shows up for you, it's a nudge to return to present moment awareness and show appreciation and gratitude for the people or pets in your life who are loyal and steadfast. It's also a good time to assess where your loyalties lie and how these relationships serve you and those involved.

SOUL PLAY

Essential Oil

Geranium

Crystal

Aventurine

Repeat this **Chakra Mantra**
for 30 seconds:

YAM (Y-A-A-A-M)

Repeat this **Affirmation**
three times:

I value loyalty in relationships.

Journal Prompt

What does loyalty mean to you?

~

SOUL STUDY

Journal Prompt

You have remained loyal to a person, a job, an ideal when that loyalty no longer served you. How can you learn to let go in those situations?

Defining Moments

Agape ~ Covenant

28

Island Unto Thyself

Solitude ~ Sovereignty ~ Interdependence

~

Community

Heart Chakra

~

The Oracle Message

If you feel isolated and your loved ones are not available, choose solitude. Isolation is lonely. Solitude is chosen. You can be alone by choice and still hold your place within the greater collective. Relish your time with yourself. You are your connection to others but you are also your connection to yourself.

SOUL PLAY

Essential Oil

Geranium

Crystal

Aventurine

Repeat this **Chakra Mantra**
for 30 seconds:

YAM (Y-A-A-A-M)

Repeat this **Affirmation**
three times:

I treasure solitude.

Journal Prompt

How does alone time refuel you?

~

SOUL STUDY

Journal Prompt

When you experience loneliness, what fears well up in you?

Defining Moments

Self-reliance ~ Walden Pond

29

Honor Your Temple

Organic ~ Sustainable ~ Holistic

Nourishment
Solar Plexus Chakra

The Oracle Message

Be mindful not just about what you feed your body, be mindful also of what you put on and around your body. Your body is your temple. Fresh, organic food, non-toxic personal care products and green cleaning products are essential. Eat clean, breathe clean, live clean.

SOUL PLAY

Essential Oil

Juniper

Crystal

Tiger Eye

Repeat this **Chakra Mantra** for 30 seconds:

RAM (R-A-A-A-M)

Repeat this **Affirmation** three times:

I embrace a wellness lifestyle.

Journal Prompt

In what ways are you honoring your temple well?

~

SOUL STUDY

Journal Prompt

What are ways you can better respect your temple?

Defining Moments

Chemical Fragrance ~ Green Living

30

You Are What You Eat

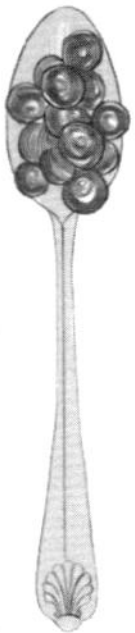

Quality ~ Discernment ~ Sustenance

~

Nourishment

Solar Plexus Chakra

~

The Oracle Message

What you take into your body, brain and soul matters. "Diet" is derived from the Latin "diaeta" which means "way of life." Food is fuel. It is what sustains our bodies to continue regular functioning. Choosing high quality foods for our bodies, high quality information for our brains and high quality interactions for our souls is key to an optimal "way of life."

SOUL PLAY

Essential Oil

Juniper

Crystal

Tiger Eye

Repeat this **Chakra Mantra** for 30 seconds:

RAM (R-A-A-A-M)

Repeat this **Affirmation** three times:

I choose a high quality diet for my body, brain and soul.

Journal Prompt

Describe a food, an information source and a social interaction that nourishes you.

~

SOUL STUDY

Journal Prompt

What part of your body, brain, soul diet needs adjusting?

Defining Moments

Gut/Brain Connection ~ Non-GMO

31

Hungry Ghost

Mindful ~ Intentional ~ Satiated

~

Nourishment

Solar Plexus Chakra

~

The Oracle Message

When you eat with reckless abandon, you are feeding the hungry ghost. Instead, be intentional about what you eat and how you eat. Take mindful bites of food and savor the experience. Every meal and snack is a blessing. Approach everything in life with simple bites.

SOUL PLAY

Essential Oil

Juniper

Crystal

Tiger Eye

Repeat this **Chakra Mantra** for 30 seconds:

RAM (R-A-A-A-M)

Repeat this **Affirmation** three times:

I savor each moment of life.

Journal Prompt

Give examples of savoring food and life in small bites.

~

SOUL STUDY

Journal Prompt

When have you fed the hungry ghost?

Defining Moments

Mindful Eating ~ Intuitive Eating

32

Seat of the Soul

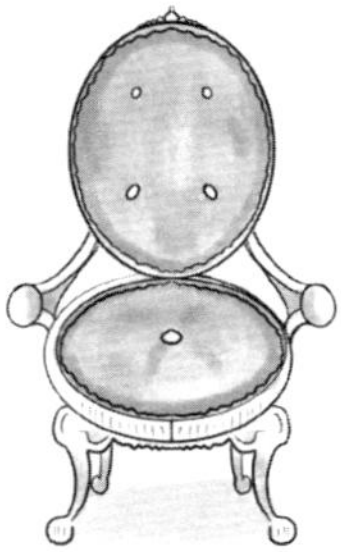

Guidance ~ Ambition ~ Determination

Nourishment

Solar Plexus Chakra

The Oracle Message

When you feel your gut twist, that is your inner GPS system guiding you. You are encouraged to be the authority of your own life. Know your worth and when you feel fire in the belly know that your ambition and determination is noteworthy. Your sense of purpose sits at the seat of your soul.

SOUL PLAY

Essential Oil

Juniper

Crystal

Tiger Eye

Repeat this **Chakra Mantra** for 30 seconds:

RAM (R-A-A-A-M)

Repeat this **Affirmation** three times:

I can do everything that I desire

Journal Prompt

Describe your motivation when it comes from the fire within you.

~

SOUL STUDY

Journal Prompt

What situations cause you to doubt your abilities and quell your motivation?

Defining Moments

Personal Drive ~ Fire in the Belly

33

Mirror, Mirror

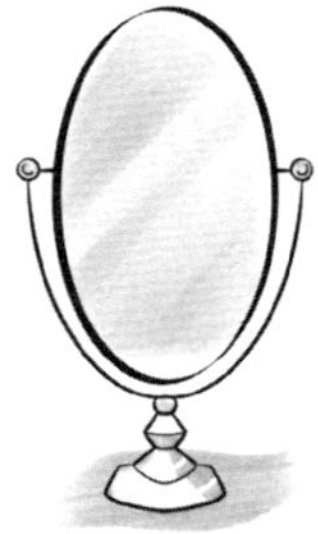

Reflection ~ Perception ~ Reaction

~

Nourishment

Solar Plexus Chakra

~

The Oracle Message

It has been said that the eyes are the window to one's soul. What do you see when you look into the eyes of another? This is a time to be reflective of the relationships in your life, romantic or otherwise. What you see is being mirrored back to you for a reason. What bubbles up is what calls out for attention. When you take charge at your core, your belly settles and you feel your worth.

SOUL PLAY

Essential Oil

Juniper

Crystal

Tiger Eye

Repeat this **Chakra Mantra**
for 30 seconds:

RAM (R-A-A-A-M)

Repeat this **Affirmation**
three times:

I am worthy of love, kindness, and respect

Journal Prompt

When you look into the eyes of someone you love, what do you see?

~

SOUL STUDY

Journal Prompt

What is the core issue being reflected back to you from another right now?

Defining Moments

Soul Mate ~ Twin Flame

34

All In the Details

Synchronicity ~ Observation ~ Focus

Nourishment

Solar Plexus Chakra

The Oracle Message

When Mouse makes a visit, it is a nudge to get laser-focused on a situation or to pay close attention to the synchronicities that are happening around you. See beyond the superficiality of life and follow your gut based on the details that you are shown.

SOUL PLAY

Essential Oil

Juniper

Crystal

Tiger Eye

Repeat this **Chakra Mantra** for 30 seconds:

RAM (R-A-A-A-M)

Repeat this **Affirmation** three times:

I use my keen eye and gut responses as I go about each day with confidence.

Journal Prompt

What synchronicities have appeared to you lately? What do they symbolize to you?

~

SOUL STUDY

Journal Prompt

Pay attention to your resistance in tracking synchronicities. What are you really resisting?

Defining Moments

Acausal Parallelism ~ Meaningful Coincidence

35

Pat On the Back

Meaning ~ Worth ~ Purpose

~

Nourishment

Solar Plexus Chakra

~

The Oracle Message

We all have times when we wonder about the meaning of life. Meaninglessness is defined as one of the four existential crises. Remember that everything holds a vibration and has meaning. Your life has purpose and you are worthy. Give yourself a pat on the back.

SOUL PLAY

Essential Oil

Juniper

Crystal

Tiger Eye

Repeat this **Chakra Mantra**
for 30 seconds:

RAM (R-A-A-A-M)

Repeat this **Affirmation**
three times:

*My joyous life is meaningful
and purposeful.*

Journal Prompt

*What is meaningful and valuable
in your life?*

~

SOUL STUDY

Journal Prompt

*What situations cause you to feel
unworthy of a joyous and meaningful life?*

Defining Moments

Eudaimonia ~ Nirvana

36
Tabula Rasa

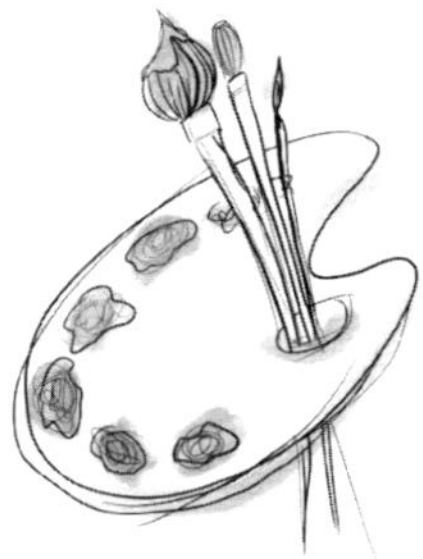

Co-creation ~ Design ~ Renewal

~

Creativity
Sacral Chakra

~

The Oracle Message

Each day, we're given the privilege of beginning anew. Every new 24 hours is a blank canvas to co-create the life we desire. Let your passion guide you as you paint your world with all the colors available from Spirit.

SOUL PLAY

Essential Oil

Vetiver

Crystal

Carnelian

Repeat this **Chakra Mantra** for 30 seconds:

VAM (V-A-A-A-M)

Repeat this **Affirmation** three times:

I am a passionate co-creator and design my life on my terms.

Journal Prompt

Draw a picture (no skill level required) of your best life.

~

SOUL STUDY

Journal Prompt

If you could use the eraser, what would you edit out of your current life?

Defining Moments

Mind Map ~ Focus Wheel

37
Respect Your Mother

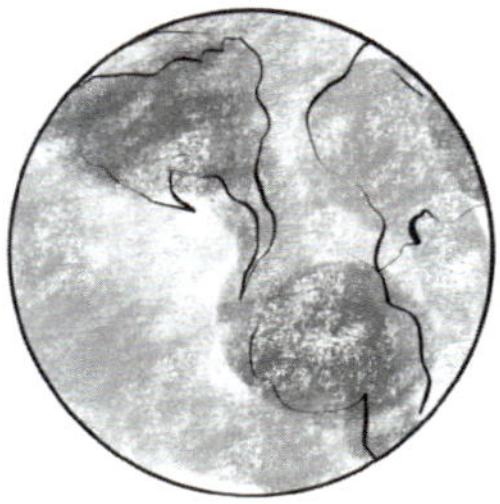

Earth ~ Sacredness ~ Symbiosis

Creativity
Sacral Chakra

The Oracle Message

You are a part of an Earth family. Mama Gaia holds you in her loving arms, providing you with a sacred space to imagine, design and build the life you desire. This is a symbiotic relationship. Find ways to support the Earth and make your mark, so the planet and its inhabitants are left better than when you arrived.

SOUL PLAY

Essential Oil

Vetiver

Crystal

Carnelian

Repeat this **Chakra Mantra**
for 30 seconds:

VAM (V-A-A-A-M)

Repeat this **Affirmation**
three times:

I add value to myself and the planet each day.

Journal Prompt

How have you contributed to the betterment of Earth?

~

SOUL STUDY

Journal Prompt

What can you discard or recycle that would improve your life and others'?

Defining Moments

Gaia ~ Pachamama

38

Sovereign Connection

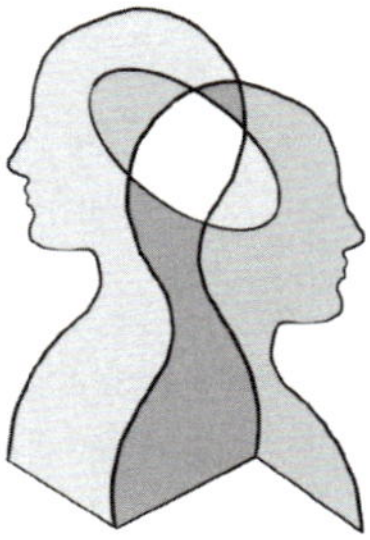

Mutuality ~ Romance ~ Passion

Creativity

Sacral Chakra

The Oracle Message

Romantic love is often rooted in sacral desire. A healthy relationship with your lover is sovereign and interdependent. Addiction and/or codependence often shows up when the relationship is not balanced. Be engaged in healthy love with self or others that includes both respect and passion.

SOUL PLAY

Essential Oil

Vetiver

Crystal

Carnelian

Repeat this **Chakra Mantra** for 30 seconds:

VAM (V-A-A-A-M)

Repeat this **Affirmation** three times:

My love relationships are balanced and healthy.

Journal Prompt

Describe your perfect relationship.

~

SOUL STUDY

Journal Prompt

When have you experienced an unbalanced romance?

Defining Moments

Limerence ~ Eros

39

Rising Up

Vibration ~ Sensuality ~ Transmutation

~

Creativity

Sacral Chakra

~

The Oracle Message

When Kundalini Rising happens it is a rising up. You feel more creative, sensual and sexual. The energy that pours forth from you is sacred and tantric. Your spine tingles and your vibration is palpable. Your frequency is tuned in to the Greater Good and you are able to transmute.

SOUL PLAY

Essential Oil

Vetiver

Crystal

Carnelian

Repeat this **Chakra Mantra** for 30 seconds:

VAM (V-A-A-A-M)

Repeat this **Affirmation** three times:

I embrace sacred sensuality.

Journal Prompt

Describe a time when creativity felt "tingly" and exhilarating.

~

SOUL STUDY

Journal Prompt

What hinders your creative process?

Defining Moments

Kundalini Rising ~ Tantra

40
All Work and No Play

Balance ~ Fun ~ Function

~

Creativity
Sacral Chakra

~

The Oracle Message
Responsibility. This single word has such weight to it, doesn't it? Sure, we have a responsibility to complete tasks, pay bills, tend to family matters, etc. However, we also have a responsibility to not just decompress and de-stress, but to relax and recreate, revel and romp. Balance is key. Find ways to enjoy your work, but also find time to just go goof off and frolic.

SOUL PLAY

Essential Oil

Vetiver

Crystal

Carnelian

Repeat this **Chakra Mantra** for 30 seconds:

VAM (V-A-A-A-M)

Repeat this **Affirmation** three times:

I always have enough time to have fun and enjoy life.

Journal Prompt

What did you love doing as a kid that made you lose track of time?

~

SOUL STUDY

Journal Prompt

What un-fun task do you spend the most time doing each week that you could delegate?

Defining Moments

Work-Life Balance ~ Wellness Wheel

41

In Motion

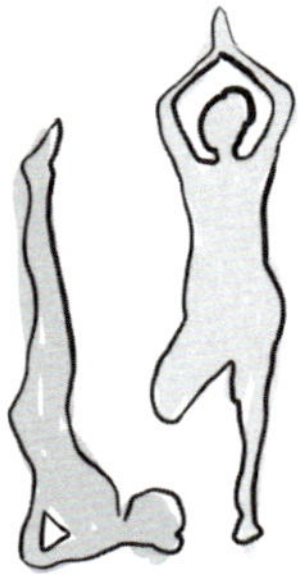

Physicality ~ Movement ~ Momentum

~

Creativity

Sacral Chakra

~

The Oracle Message

Get moving and grooving! When your mind has been doing a lot of work, adding in body movement will help your ideas reach another level of momentum. A body in motion stays in motion. Get creative and get your blood flowing. This can help you transmute mental energy into tangible results.

SOUL PLAY

Essential Oil

Vetiver

Crystal

Carnelian

Repeat this **Chakra Mantra** for 30 seconds:

VAM (V-A-A-A-M)

Repeat this **Affirmation** three times:

I turn mental and physical energy into manifested goals.

Journal Prompt

When your body is in motion, what are the positive rewards?

~

SOUL STUDY

Journal Prompt

What keeps your body stagnant and stuck?

Defining Moments

Newton's Laws of Motion ~ Transmuting Energy

42

Yes, Please

Pleasure ~ Gifts ~ Indulgence

~

Creativity
Sacral Chakra

~

The Oracle Message

The sacral chakra is your pleasure center. Saying yes to life and indulging in the small and big things—that's what this is about. Bring on the pleasure you deserve and receive delight like a gift from a dear friend. Allow the gratification to spark your passion and creativity!

SOUL PLAY

Essential Oil

Vetiver

Crystal

Carnelian

Repeat this **Chakra Mantra** for 30 seconds:

VAM (V-A-A-A-M)

Repeat this **Affirmation** three times:

I welcome gifts from the Universe.

Journal Prompt

What can you indulge in today to experience life's simple pleasures?

~

SOUL STUDY

Journal Prompt

What gifts have you turned down in the past?

Defining Moments

Pleasure Principle ~ Cornucopia

43

The Anointed One

Earthy ~ Vibrant ~ Blissful

~

Sanctuary

Root Chakra

~

The Oracle Message

Essential oils are vibrant and terrestrial. Be anointed and experience spiritual bliss. Samadhi, Enlightenment, Christ Consciousness—Oneness can be yours. Allow the oils to ground you starting at your root chakra. Move up your astral spine anointing each chakra through to your crown. Your chakras are balanced now. You are ready to experience higher consciousness.

SOUL PLAY

Essential Oil

Cypress

Crystal

Red Jasper

Repeat this **Chakra Mantra**
for 30 seconds:

LAM (L-A-A-A-M)

Repeat this **Affirmation**
three times:

I am deeply rooted.

Journal Prompt

Envision the cypress tree with roots reaching down to middle earth. Write about feeling as grounded as the cypress tree.

~

SOUL STUDY

Journal Prompt

Describe a time that you felt like a tall tree with a shallow root bed.

Defining Moments

Aromatherapy ~ Sacred Attar

44

Whence You Came

Lineage ~ Family ~ History

Sanctuary

Root Chakra

The Oracle Message

Day of the Dead is a Mexican celebration that honors ancestors and saints. Touching history, we are influenced by those who came before us. We are part of a lineage that has woven its thread through our history and our lives. Celebrate those who came before you, whether they are related by DNA or adopted by you along your journey into your soul family.

SOUL PLAY

Essential Oil

Cypress

Crystal

Red Jasper

Repeat this **Chakra Mantra**
for 30 seconds:

LAM (L-A-A-A-M)

Repeat this **Affirmation**
three times:

I honor my roots and celebrate the life I've chosen.

Journal Prompt

Which ancestor or older family member has made a positive impression on your life?

~

SOUL STUDY

Journal Prompt

Who in your family tree are you having a difficult time honoring?

Defining Moments

All Saints Day ~ All Souls Day

45

Glass Half Full

Abundance ~ Allowing ~ Receiving

~

Sanctuary
Root Chakra

~

The Oracle Message

There is always enough for everyone—enough resources, enough access, enough sustainability, enough joy, enough love. However, it is up to us to ask, allow and receive all the goodness life is offering us each day. Shift into a state of allowing and get ready for the goodness to fill up your cup!

SOUL PLAY

Essential Oil

Cypress

Crystal

Red Jasper

Repeat this **Chakra Mantra** for 30 seconds:

LAM (L-A-A-A-M)

Repeat this **Affirmation** three times:

I am enough. I have enough. I give enough.

Journal Prompt

Reflect on a time when you received a blessing or gift.

~

SOUL STUDY

Journal Prompt

Describe a time when being grateful has been difficult.

Defining Moments

Abraham Channeled ~ Law of Attraction

46

Feet In the Dirt

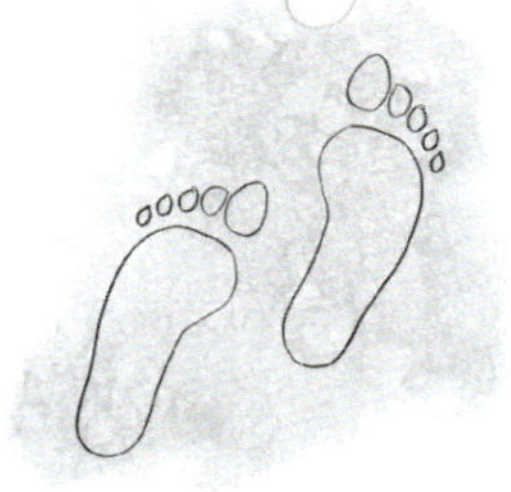

Nature ~ Roots ~ Connectedness

~

Sanctuary

Root Chakra

~

The Oracle Message

Plant your feet in the dirt. Connect to Mother Earth. Go for a walk in the forest. Forest bathing is so soothing for the soul. While you are in the forest, pay attention to how the roots of the trees intertwine in a perfect connectedness. Place your hands on the tree's trunk. Feel yourself being one with nature.

SOUL PLAY

Essential Oil

Cypress

Crystal

Red Jasper

Repeat this **Chakra Mantra** for 30 seconds:

LAM (L-A-A-A-M)

Repeat this **Affirmation** three times:

I am supported by Mother Gaia.

Journal Prompt

Write about what it feels like to touch the earth—placing your feet in the dirt or creating a snow angel. . .

~

SOUL STUDY

Journal Prompt

Describe the times you feel disconnected from nature and consequently, disconnected from others.

Defining Moments

Earthing ~ Forest Bathing

47

Healing Waters

Hydrate ~ Soak ~ Replenish

~

Sanctuary
Root Chakra

~

The Oracle Message

H2O. Our bodies are approximately 60% water. We not only survive, but thrive because of the healing power of water. Using water to rinse off the events of the day, warm yourself up, cool yourself down, or simply soak in the minerals that nature provides us can soothe your soul, calm your nerves and nourish your body. Let water replenish your spirit.

SOUL PLAY

Essential Oil

Cypress

Crystal

Red Jasper

Repeat this **Chakra Mantra**
for 30 seconds:

LAM (L-A-A-A-M)

Repeat this **Affirmation**
three times:

I soak in all the goodness life has to offer.

Journal Prompt

*Reflect on a positive memory
that involves water.*

~

SOUL STUDY

Journal Prompt

What is your soul thirsty for?

Defining Moments

Hydrotherapy ~ Holy Water

48

Spa Day

Luxuriate ~ Pamper ~ Bask

~

Sanctuary

Root Chakra

~

The Oracle Message

You are worth it! Take time for self-care. Pamper yourself. Give yourself an entire day just to focus on you. Whether you go to the spa or create your own in-home spa; whether you get your crayons and coloring book out, or go to an art class, make it all about you! Self-care equals grounding and stability.

SOUL PLAY

Essential Oil

Cypress

Crystal

Red Jasper

Repeat this **Chakra Mantra** for 30 seconds:

LAM (L-A-A-A-M)

Repeat this **Affirmation** three times:

I nurture myself and take care of my well-being.

Journal Prompt

Describe how you feel when you bask in your own delights.

~

SOUL STUDY

Journal Prompt

What keeps you from indulging and giving yourself me-time?

Defining Moments

Self-Care ~ Eustress

49

Map It Out

Alignment ~ Integration ~ Direction

~

Sanctuary

Root Chakra

~

The Oracle Message

Navigate your life story as a soul journey towards personal integration. You live in two worlds—the finite, concrete dimension of your outer life and the infinite, intangible dimension of your inner life. Find your guide at the crossroads to help you map it out.

SOUL PLAY

Essential Oil

Cypress

Crystal

Red Jasper

Repeat this **Chakra Mantra** for 30 seconds:

LAM (L-A-A-A-M)

Say this **Affirmation** three times:

As above, so below. I am anchored and guided by source.

Journal Prompt

Describe a time when you trusted Spirit to guide you down the right path.

~

SOUL STUDY

Journal Prompt

When you are at the fork in the road, what keeps you from trusting your inner GPS?

Defining Moments

4Fold Path ~ InnerView Guidance

About the Authors

DeeAnna Merz Nagel is a licensed psychotherapist, board certified coach and aromatherapist. She integrates energy healing and intuition as well as chakra balancing and essential oils into her work with others. Her greatest passion is guiding people toward their soul's purpose. Her background includes a M.Ed. in Rehabilitation Counseling and a B.S. in Mental Health and Human Services. She holds several credentials in the healing arts. DeeAnna completed her doctorate (D.Th) with a focus on Spiritual Direction.

deeannamerznagel.com

♥

Madison Leigh Akridge is a licensed psychotherapist and board certified coach. Her background includes a BA in philosophy and Master of Social Work (MSW). Madison is also a Reiki Master/Teacher, Life Coach Trainer, Poet, and has training and certifications in a variety of energy/wellness modalities. She uses an array of intuitive tools in her work and assists others in exploring their soul's vision, values, and purpose. Madison is currently completing her doctorate (D.Th) with a focus on Spiritual Direction.

madisonleighakridge.com

♥

essentialsoul.care

♥

About the Artist

Lia Littlewood is a Yuma, AZ native who loves creating avenues for artists to reach their potential. Littlewood has been nominated twice for the Governors art award, statewide, and won the Tribute of the Muses in 2017, highest art award in the city of Yuma. She is a renowned artist who has made her mark on Yuma and its rich local art scene, whether it be on canvas, a sculpture or a captivating mural. Littlewood's art reaches far and wide. Her talent is captured here in black and white illustrations, bringing the Oracle's messages to life.

lialittlewood.com

♥

More Flower of Life Press books

Check out additional books at **flowerofliferess.com**